THE ARCHITECT SAYS

Published by
Princeton Architectural Press
37 East 7th Street, New York, NY 10003
Visit our website at www.papress.com

PAPress Editor: Sara Bader
Designers: Paul Wagner and Jan Haux

Special thanks to: Bree Anne Apperley, Nicola Bednarek Brower, Janet Behning,
Fannie Bushin, Megan Carey, Carina Cha, Andrea Chlad, Russell Fernandez,
Will Foster, Diane Levinson, Jennifer Lippert, Jacob Moore, Gina Morrow,
Katharine Myers, Margaret Rogalski, Elana Schlenker, Dan Simon, Sara Stemen,
Andrew Stepanian, and Joseph Weston of Princeton Architectural Press
—Kevin C. Lippert, publisher

Library of Congress Cataloging-in-Publication Data
The architect says : quotes, quips, and words of wisdom / compiled and
edited by Laura S. Dushkes. — First edition.
    pages   cm
ISBN 978-1-61689-093-3 (hardcover : alk. paper)
1. Architecture—Quotations. 2. Architects—Quotations. I. Dushkes,
Laura S., 1960–
PN6084.A75A73 2012
808.88'2—dc23

                                             2012012426

the
ARCHITECT
says

Quotes, Quips, and Words of Wisdom

compiled and edited by Laura S. Dushkes

I am the librarian for an architectural firm based in Seattle. As part of my job, I have the good fortune to shop for, select, and handle beautiful books on the works of architects from around the world. How many people are paid to wander through a bookstore and choose books to buy and share with colleagues? The architects I work with eagerly pore over the latest additions to our library, calling out particular photographs and images that speak to them.

But it's the language that speaks to me. When I look through a book, a sentence might jump out at me. Sometimes it's just a word.

A few years ago I started collecting those words, so I could assemble them in a book. I wanted to show the depth and breadth of the thinking of architects through time, how they may all grapple with a core set of issues, but their approaches and opinions can vary wildly.

I have tried to include thoughts of leading architects working today (Wang Shu was awarded the 2012 Pritzker Prize just days before my manuscript was due), as well as voices from the past, among them Vitruvius, Leonardo da Vinci, and Palladio. I have selected one quotation per page, each pairing, or spread, creating its own self-contained mini-conversation. The architects may have lived in different eras (Richard Neutra is "seated" next to Vitruvius) or they may be contemporary colleagues inspiring each other with the built work they are designing today. Some may disagree with each other; others share the same passion for something specific (the satisfaction of a pile of "unsullied paper," for example, or the value of constraints). It is my hope that each of these exchanges illuminates what has been important to architects across the ages and around the world.

My greatest challenge in compiling this book was deciding which quotations to select from the vast pool I've collected. There are many architects, far too many to count, who are not reflected in this volume. Their absence is simply a function of space. As expressed by architects in the pages that follow, constraints can be useful, as they give us something to "work against." For this collection, choosing quotations to fit within the physical constraints of a book required a rigorous edit. There exists a deep well of thoughts, quips, and words of wisdom by architects—at the library, in bookstores, within the volumes lining your bookshelves, and embedded in lectures and interviews widely accessible on the Internet. I hope this collection inspires you to look for more.

Laura S. Dushkes

I am **deeply impressed** with the designer of the universe; I am confident I couldn't have done anywhere near such a good job.

Buckminster Fuller (1895–1983)

A profound design process eventually makes the patron, the architect, and every occasional visitor in the building **a slightly better human being.**

Juhani Pallasmaa (1936–)

I've said goodbye to the **overworked notion** that architecture has to save the world.

Peter Zumthor (1943–)

We do not create the work. I believe we, in fact, are discoverers.

Glenn Murcutt (1936–)

*For me, every day is a new thing. I approach each project with a new insecurity, almost like the first project I ever did, and I get the sweats, I go in and start working, **I'm not sure where I'm going**—if I knew where I was going, I wouldn't do it.*

Frank Gehry (1929–)

I pick up my pen. It flows. A building appears. There it is. There is nothing more to say.

Oscar Niemeyer (1907–)

To me the drawn language is a very revealing language: one can see in a few lines whether a man is really an architect.

Eero Saarinen (1910–61)

IS ANYTHING MORE PLEASURABLE TO THE MIND THAN UNSULLIED PAPER? THE STUDIOUS COMPARISONS AND SELECTION OF "STOCK" IN TEXTURES AND COLORS OF CARDS AND PAPER?

Frank Lloyd Wright (1867–1959)

I LOVE PAPER. A NICE THICK PILE OF IT AND A PENCIL, AND I'M CONTENT.

Cecil Balmond (1943–)

I prefer drawing to talking. Drawing is faster, and leaves less room for lies.

Le Corbusier (1887–1965)

I've noticed the computer sometimes leads to rather bland decision making; now, anybody can do a wobbly, blobby building.

Peter Cook (1936–)

I THINK DRAWINGS
ARE DRAWINGS AND
BUILDINGS ARE BUILDINGS.
WHEN I DRAW, I TRY
TO REPRESENT THE IDEA
OF THE BUILDING.
THE DRAWINGS, HOWEVER,
ARE IN WATERCOLOR,
OR PRISMACOLOR,
OR GRAPHITE ON PAPER,
AND THEREFORE THEY
CANNOT BE A BUILDING.

Michael Graves (1934–)

Architects make drawings that other people build. I make the drawings. If someone wants to build from those, that's up to them.

Lebbeus Woods (1940–)

I tell my students: you must put into your work first effort, second love, and third suffering.

Glenn Murcutt (1936–)

I make a project and I panic. Which is good, it can be a method. First, panic. Second, conquer panic by working. Third, find ways to solve your doubts.

Eduardo Souto de Moura (1952–)

For a long time Friedrich Achleitner thought about whether he wanted to be a poet or an architect, and then he shaved his head, put on a straw hat, and said he was a poet. And he said he had to decide: architecture or literature. And then I said: You could also decide to do architecture and literature. And after several years that's what he decided to do.

Hans Hollein (1934–)

After studying
art and then studying
architecture, I never
needed the clarity
of either being a
professional architect
or being an artist,
and found some
kind of middle ground
that was contaminated
from all sides.

Elizabeth Diller (1954–)

There are many architects
who aren't really aware
of their own patterns, just
like most people don't know
their patterns in private.
We find that a really exciting
theme because architecture
and psychology suddenly
become very close.

Jacques Herzog (1950–)

I've always felt that the most important thing is **finding a way of escaping the framework** or aesthetic consciousness with which I am burdened.

Arata Isozaki (1931–)

Beauty will result from the form and correspondence of the whole, with respect to the several parts, of the parts with regard to each other, and of these again to the whole; that the structure may appear an entire and complete body, wherein each member agrees with the other, and all are necessary to compose what you intend to form.

Andrea Palladio (1508–80)

I don't design nice buildings—I don't like them. I like architecture to have some raw, vital, earthy quality. You don't need to make concrete perfectly smooth or paint it or polish it. If you consider changes in the play of light on a building before it's built, you can vary the color and feel of concrete by daylight alone.

Zaha Hadid (1950–)

IN PURE ARCHITECTURE THE SMALLEST DETAIL SHOULD HAVE A MEANING OR SERVE A PURPOSE.

A. W. N. Pugin (1812–52)

Remember that the most beautiful things in the world are the most useless; peacocks and lilies, for instance.

John Ruskin* (1819–1900)

*Critic

I don't want to
undress architecture.
I want to enrich it
and add layers to it.
Basically like in
a Gothic cathedral,
where the ornament
and the structure
form an alliance.

Cecil Balmond (1943–)

My goal is to strip things down, not so that they become inhuman but so that you need just the right amount of words or shape to convey what you need to convey. I like editing.

Maya Lin (1959–)

Less is more.

Ludwig Mies van der Rohe (1886–1969)

LESS IS A BORE.

Robert Venturi (1925–)

There is a generic quality to white that we like.

Kazuyo Sejima (1956–)

Ornamentation has been,
is, and will be polychrome.
**Nature does not present us
with an object in monochrome,**
totally uniform with respect
to color–not in vegetation,
not in geology, not in topography,
not in the animal kingdom.
Always the contrast of color
is more or less lively, and for
this reason we must color wholly
or in part every architectural
element.

Antoni Gaudí (1852–1926)

I always try to think in curves.

Greg Lynn (1964–)

The worker destined to fashion hoops, to curve the wood of the forests, will offer to the great ones of the earth a monumental idea, and teach them that nothing is to be neglected for high conceptions. Is not the workshop of the world inscribed in a circle?

Claude-Nicolas Ledoux (1736–1806)

Form ever follows function.

Louis Sullivan (1856–1924)

Form follows form, not function.

Philip Johnson (1906–2005)

At the time form follows function was coined, how a building became three-dimensional was programmatic. **Many other things now come into play:** environment, costs, time, qualitative aspects of the building's materiality. This is a very different alchemy than form following function.

James Timberlake (1952–)

"Form follows profit" is the aesthetic principle of our times.

Richard Rogers (1933–)

Walter Gropius came to see me at my house at Canoas above Rio. I designed it in a sequence of natural curves to flow in and out of the existing landscape. He said, it's beautiful, but it can't be mass-produced. As if I had intended such a thing! What an idiot.

Oscar Niemeyer (1907–)

A product often becomes **more useful if the costs are lowered** without harming the quality.

Charles Eames (1907–78)

In furniture design the basic problem from a historical— and practical—point of view is the connecting element between the vertical and horizontal pieces. I believe this is absolutely decisive in giving the style its character. And when joining with the horizontal level, **the chair leg is the little sister of the architectonic column.**

Alvar Aalto (1898–1976)

A chair is a very difficult object. A skyscraper is almost easier. That is why Chippendale is famous.

Ludwig Mies van der Rohe (1886–1969)

The skyscraper is Olympian or Orwellian, depending on how you look at it.... It romanticizes power and the urban condition and celebrates leverage and cash flow. Its less romantic side effects are greed and chaos writ monstrously large.

Ada Louise Huxtable* (1921–)

*Critic

THE DESIRE TO REACH FOR THE SKY RUNS VERY DEEP IN OUR HUMAN PSYCHE.

Cesar Pelli (1926–)

I'll plan anything a man wants, from **a cathedral to a chicken coop.** That's the way I make my living.

Henry Hobson Richardson (1838–86)

Don't ever turn down a job because it's beneath you.

Julia Morgan (1872–1957)

The ideal project does not exist, each time there is the opportunity to realize an approximation.

Paulo Mendes da Rocha (1928–)

When an
architect is
asked what
his best
building is,
he usually
answers,
"The next one."

Emilio Ambasz (1943–)

IF AN ARCHITECT'S EGO IS VERY SMALL, HE IS DONE FOR; IF IT IS VAST THEN HE MIGHT MAKE SOME VERY IMPORTANT CONTRIBUTIONS.

Paolo Soleri (1919–)

Beware of over- confidence; especially in matters of structure.

Cass Gilbert (1859–1934)

I've been accused of saying I was the greatest architect in the world and if I had said so, I don't think it would be very arrogant, because I don't believe there are many—if any.

Frank Lloyd Wright (1867–1959)

I MAY NOT BE THE
MOST INTERESTING
ARCHITECT, BUT I'M STILL
OUT THERE AND HAVE
MAINTAINED SOME
POSITION OF INTEGRITY.

David Chipperfield (1953–)

I'm totally against the heroic stuff. We do little stuff. We are totally for the pathetic.

Michael Meredith (1971–)

Basically, the idea is that with everyone striving to be revolutionary, **you will be most revolutionary** if you try to be ordinary.

Denise Scott Brown (1931–)

The best form is
there already and
no one should be afraid
of using it, even if the
basic idea for it comes
from someone else.
Enough of our geniuses
and their originality.

Adolf Loos (1870–1933)

If you think you can't make the world a better place with your work, at least make sure you don't make it worse.

Herman Hertzberger (1932–)

I NEVER USE ANY IDEAS AGAIN. ONCE I'VE USED THEM, THAT'S IT.

Arthur Erickson (1924–2009)

It's not a sign of creativity to have sixty-five ideas for one problem. It's just a waste of energy.

Jan Kaplický (1937–2009)

Something as common as house paint can be exciting when polished to a mirror finish.

Tod Williams (1943–)

It is against
a white surface
that one best
appreciates
the play of light
and shadow,
solids and voids.

Richard Meier (1934–)

LIGHT IS NOT
SOMETHING VAGUE,
DIFFUSED, WHICH
IS TAKEN FOR GRANTED
BECAUSE IT IS ALWAYS
THERE. THE SUN
DOES NOT RISE EVERY
DAY IN VAIN.

Alberto Campo Baeza (1946–)

Each material has its own shadow. The shadow of stone is not the same as that of a brittle autumn leaf. The shadow penetrates the material and radiates its message.

Sverre Fehn (1924–2009)

The sun never knew how great it was until it hit the side of a building.

Louis Kahn (1901–74)

I am always searching for more light and space.

Santiago Calatrava (1951–)

ARCHITECTURE IS
BOUND TO SITUATION.
AND I FEEL LIKE
**THE SITE IS A
METAPHYSICAL LINK,
A POETIC LINK,**
TO WHAT A BUILDING
CAN BE.

Steven Holl (1947–)

The design of buildings in natural settings, whether urban or rural, must be responsive to the earth out of which they arise and the sky against which they are seen.

James Polshek (1930–)

From where stems the idea that our streets should look as if they were created by the same client or the same architect? Diversity, and not its opposite, is amusing.

Günter Behnisch (1922–2010)

Inconsistency itself breeds vitality.

Kenzo Tange (1913–2005)

YOU CAN PUT DOWN A BAD BOOK; YOU CAN AVOID LISTENING TO BAD MUSIC; BUT YOU CANNOT MISS THE UGLY TOWER BLOCK OPPOSITE YOUR HOUSE.

Renzo Piano (1937–)

It is perfectly reasonable to talk about the meaning of literature without talking about Danielle Steel, but **can you grapple with the impact of architecture without looking at Main Street?**

Paul Goldberger* (1950–)

*Critic

I believe that **context is an incredibly overestimated word and alibi** for a lot of operations. There is only one kind of architectural context between two things that are of equivalent size or value. It's very important for us to liberate ourselves from the notion of having respect for context, as a kind of reflex, an automatism. We have to be more skeptical about context.

Rem Koolhaas (1944–)

I am always surprised by how much little emphasis schools of architecture, and indeed, many architects, place on the process of the mating of a building.

Norman Foster (1935–)

You cannot simply put something new into a place. You have to **absorb what you see around you**, *what exists on the land, and then use that knowledge along with contemporary thinking to interpret what you see.*

Tadao Ando (1941–)

I'm not going to say that someone like Frank Gehry can't build something beautiful in a culture and place he doesn't know well. For the rest of us mere mortals, **the best way to make real architecture is by letting a building evolve out of the culture and place.**

Samuel Mockbee (1944–2001)

For fortified towns the following general principles are to be observed. **First comes the choice of a very healthy site.** Such a site will be high, neither misty nor frosty, and in a climate neither hot nor cold, but temperate; further, without marshes in the neighborhood. For when the morning breezes blow toward the town at sunrise, if they bring with them mists from marshes and, mingled with the mist, the poisonous breath of the creatures of the marshes to be wafted into the bodies of the inhabitants, they will make the site unhealthy.

Vitruvius (ca. 80 – ca. 15 BCE)

THE ARCHITECT WHO REALLY DESIGNS FOR A HUMAN BEING HAS TO KNOW A GREAT DEAL MORE THAN JUST THE FIVE CANONS OF VITRUVIUS.

Richard Neutra (1892–1970)

I THINK BUILDINGS SHOULD IMITATE ECOLOGICAL SYSTEMS.

Ken Yeang (1948–)

What if a building were more like a nest? If it were, it would be made out of local, abundant materials. It would be specific to its site and climate. It would use minimal energy but maintain comfort. It would last just long enough and then would leave no trace. It would be just what it needed to be.

Jeanne Gang (1964–)

Architecture is the constant fight between man and nature, the fight to overwhelm nature, to possess it. **The first act of architecture is to put a stone on the ground.** *That act transforms a condition of nature into a condition of culture;* **it's a holy act.**

Mario Botta (1943–)

The act of building can be brutal. **When I build on a site in nature that is totally unspoiled, it is a fight, an attack by our culture.** In this confrontation, I strive to make a building that will make people more aware of the beauty of the setting, and when looking at the building, a hope for a new consciousness to see the beauty there as well.

Sverre Fehn (1924–2009)

I USE CHEAP MATERIALS.

Herman Hertzberger (1932–)

I believe that **the material doesn't need to be strong** to be used to build a strong structure. The strength of the structure has nothing to do with the strength of the material.

Shigeru Ban (1957–)

It does not seem likely, therefore, that the revival of the use of concrete will have any influence on the style of modern architecture properly so called.

Henry Heathcote Statham (1839–1924)

I am particularly fond of concrete, symbol of the construction progress of a whole century, submissive and strong as an elephant, monumental like stone, humble like brick.

Carlos Villanueva (1900–1975)

THERE IS A NOTION THESE DAYS THAT ARCHITECTURE IS INCREASINGLY BECOMING LIGHTER. BUT I DON'T BELIEVE IT ONE BIT. IT'S JUST AN ILLUSION OF LIGHTNESS. **BUILDINGS ARE HEAVY.** I HAVEN'T MET A BUILDING I COULD LIFT.

Tod Williams (1943–)

I am trying to counter the fixity of architectures, their stolidity, with elements that give **an ineffable, immaterial quality.**

Toyo Ito (1941–)

The facade and walls of a house, church, or palace, no matter how beautiful they may be, are only the container, the box formed by the walls; the content is the internal space.

Bruno Zevi (1918–2000)

Space, space: architects always talk about space! But creating a space is not automatically doing architecture. With the same space, you can make a masterpiece or cause a disaster.

Jean Nouvel (1945–)

*I know when I was
a kid we used to throw
the football out of
a first-floor window.
We never went to a play
space; the play space
began immediately.*
**Play was inspired, not
organized.**

Louis Kahn (1901–74)

I myself am installed in a windowless air-conditioned office, a kind of cell. My visitors are conscious of this fact, which makes them speak concisely and to the point.

Le Corbusier (1887–1965)

Never talk to a client about architecture. Talk to him about his children. That is simply good politics. He will not understand what you have to say about architecture most of the time. Most of the time the client never knows what he wants.

Ludwig Mies van der Rohe (1886–1969)

I don't know why people hire architects and then tell them what to do.

Frank Gehry (1929–)

I UNDERSTAND THAT, TODAY, SOME DEVELOPERS ARE ASKING ARCHITECTS TO DESIGN **EYE-CATCHING, ICONIC BUILDINGS.** FORTUNATELY, I'VE NOT HAD THAT KIND OF CLIENT SO FAR.

Fumihiko Maki (1928–)

Sometimes one is constrained to do things against reason in order to obey the will of the lord who ordered the building to be built.

Philibert de l'Orme (ca. 1514–70)

Here is one of the few
effective keys to the design
problem—the ability of the
designer to **recognize as many
of the constraints as possible**—
his willingness and enthusiasm
for working within these
constraints—the constraints
of price, of size, of strength,
balance, of surface, of time,
etc.; each problem has its
own peculiar list.

Charles Eames (1907–78)

I THINK CONSTRAINTS ARE VERY IMPORTANT. THEY'RE POSITIVE, BECAUSE THEY ALLOW YOU TO WORK OFF SOMETHING.

Charles Gwathmey (1938–2009)

We hated Bauhaus. It was a bad time for architecture. They just didn't have any talent. All they had were rules. Even for knives and forks they created rules. Picasso would never have accepted rules. The house is a machine? No! The mechanical is ugly. The rule is the worst thing. You just want to break it.

Oscar Niemeyer (1907–)

If you have total freedom, then you are in trouble. It's much better when you have some obligation, some discipline, some rules. When you have no rules, then you start to build your own rules.

Renzo Piano (1937–)

1. sex life
2. sleeping habits
3. pets
4. gardening
5. personal hygiene
6. protection against weather
7. hygiene in the home
8. car maintenance
9. cooking
10. heating
11. insolation
12. service

These are the only requirements to be considered when building a house.

Hannes Meyer (1889–1954)

People who build
their own home tend to
be very courageous.
These people are
curious about life.
They're thinking about
what it means to live
in a house, rather than
just buying a commodity
and making it work.

Tom Kundig (1954–)

VERY OFTEN THE OPINION OF THE CLIENTS MUST BE DISREGARDED IN THEIR OWN INTEREST.

John M. Johansen (1916–)

The pressure a client brings to bear on a project makes you distill your ideas. It's like an olive press, which comes up against the resistance of the pit and thus distills the oil.

Daniel Libeskind (1946–)

I HATE VACATIONS. IF YOU CAN BUILD BUILDINGS, WHY SIT ON THE BEACH?

Philip Johnson (1906–2005)

I AM SIMPLY
SUBMERGED IN
WORK FROM FIVE
IN THE MORNING
TO ELEVEN AT NIGHT;
ALMOST NEED
A FEW DAYS OFF
TO ESCAPE
A BREAKDOWN!

Richard Neutra (1892–1970)

We're always working with choreographers and directors, robotics experts and different kinds of scientists and researchers. We're always interested in the links and crossovers between disciplines.

Elizabeth Diller (1954–)

My wife, Lu Wenyu, and I are
the only partners in the studio.
The rest are all our students.
I sent them all home for a month
so I could work on these three
museums. But they were not on
vacation. **They all had homework
assignments: books to read on
French philosophy, Chinese
paintings to study or movies to
watch, whatever might be helpful.**
When we all got back together,
we had discussions and then began
to work again on the projects.

Wang Shu (1963–)

I cannot work and listen to Wagner at the same time, nor Mahler, nor Beethoven's late quartets. I enjoy listening to Chopin's piano music when I work.

I. M. Pei (1917–)

Beethoven's Fifth Symphony, that amazing revolution in tumult and splendor of sound built on four tones based upon a rhythm a child could play on the piano with one finger. Supreme imagination reared the four repeated tones, simple rhythms, into a great symphonic poem that is **probably the noblest thought-built edifice in our world.**

Frank Lloyd Wright (1867–1959)

Children should be introduced right from the start to the potentialities of their environment, to the physical and psychological laws that govern the visual world, and to the supreme enjoyment that comes from participating in the creative process of giving form to one's living space.

Walter Gropius (1883–1969)

Every child likes to take a pencil to make a mark. Everybody makes beautiful things when they are three, four, or five years old. Most people lose that spontaneity; I think that always happens. Some are able to win a second spontaneity.

Alvaro Siza (1933–)

There is a rumor that
I can't draw and never
could. This is probably
because I work so
much with models.
Models are one of the
most beautiful design
tools, but I still do
the finest drawings
you can imagine.

Jørn Utzon (1918–2008)

I prefer to work with the looseness of pencil rather than the precision of ink or a computer.

Thom Mayne (1944–)

Drawing architecture is a "schizoid" act: it involves reducing the world to a piece of paper.

Eduardo Souto de Moura (1952–)

Many people notice that computers have their limits. I've nothing against them, but my experience with materials and forms I can touch has taken me a good deal further.

Frei Otto (1925–)

I HAVE NEVER BEEN
EMBARRASSED TO STATE
WHAT MIGHT BE SELF-
EVIDENT, SO IT WILL
COME AS NO SURPRISE
TO SUGGEST THAT THE
PENCIL AND COMPUTER
ARE, IF LEFT TO THEIR
OWN DEVICES, EQUALLY
DUMB AND ONLY AS
GOOD AS THE PERSON
DRIVING THEM.

Norman Foster (1935–)

Have you seen the plans for Bilbao? They are incredibly beautiful. You cannot draw that by hand— it has to be done with software.... I have always believed that art leads the way for architecture. **Now it is technology's turn.**

I. M. Pei (1917–)

OLD-STYLE ARCHITECTS
DID AS MUCH AS THEY
THOUGHT THEY COULD
CONTROL. THEIR OWN HAND
WAS ALWAYS INVOLVED IN
THEIR WORK; RESPONSIBILITY
WASN'T DELEGATED TO
ANYONE ELSE. ONCE WORK
IS DELEGATED AND NOT
FOLLOWED THROUGH BY THE
ORIGINAL HAND, IT'S NOT
ARCHITECTURE ANYMORE.
IT'S SOMETHING ELSE.

John Hejduk (1929–2000)

I use structural
engineers. I use
mechanical engineers.
I use housing architects
to tell me how big
an apartment is
because I don't know.
How to build a
cheap apartment?
How would I know?
I'm not interested.
I have people to do that.

Philip Johnson (1906–2005)

The best engineer a few decades ago was someone who could create the most beautiful beam or structure; today it's to do a structure you cannot see or understand how it's done. It disappears and you can talk only about color, symbols, and light. **It's an aesthetic of miracle.**

Jean Nouvel (1945–)

Engineering is not a science. Science studies particular events to find general laws. Engineering design makes use of these laws to solve particular practical problems. In this it is more closely related to art or craft.

Ove Arup* (1895–1988)

*Engineer

BETWEEN 1990 AND 2000 I HAD
NO COMMISSIONS, AND I DID
NOT WANT A GOVERNMENT OR
ACADEMIC POSITION, EITHER.
I JUST WANTED TO WORK WITH
CRAFTSMEN, GAIN EXPERIENCE
ON THE GROUND, AND TAKE NO
RESPONSIBILITY FOR THE DESIGN—
ONLY FOR THE CONSTRUCTION.

Wang Shu (1963–)

A CONSTRUCTION SITE IS AN INCREDIBLY INSTRUCTIVE PLACE FOR AN ARCHITECT. I WOULD RATHER HAVE SPENT AN HOUR AT THE SAINT PETER'S BUILDING SITE IN ROME THAN HAVE READ ALL THE BOOKS WRITTEN ABOUT THAT CHURCH.

Jørn Utzon (1918–2008)

In São Paulo there
is a bar which I go to
two or three times
a week with "normal"
people, no architects,
and I prefer this.

Paulo Mendes da Rocha (1928–)

I learn more from creative people in other disciplines than *I do even from other architects because I think they have a way of looking at the world that is really important.*

Tom Kundig (1954–)

*An important value for us
is drawing together all
of the various elements of
architecture—materials, space,
form, light, color—and producing
a unified whole. We're not
at all interested in producing
a collage.* **People's lives are
the collage and you don't need
a collage on top of a collage.**
*You need to provide some
sense of wholeness so
the kaleidoscope can occur
within it.*

Billie Tsien (1949–)

WE SHOULD WORK ON
MAKING OUR WORLD
UNDERSTANDABLE AND
NOT MAKE IT MORE
CONFUSED. WHAT LOOKS
LIKE WOOD SHOULD
ALSO BE WOOD AND IRON
SHOULD REMAIN IRON.

Günter Behnisch (1922–2010)

I have interviewed
thousands and thousands
of office workers, laboriously
asking them, "What do
you want? What do you see?
What do you care about?"
and it is a very humbling
experience. I recommend
it to you when you are
practicing architecture,
to really talk and understand
and listen, because we
as architects tend not to.

Kevin Roche (1922–)

A building is hard to judge.
It takes many years to
find out whether it works.
It's not as simple as asking
the people in the office
whether they like it.
And I'm not talking about
the applause from critics or
outsiders. They're entitled
to have an opinion—but
how can they judge how
comfortable a building is?

Helmut Jahn (1940–)

Architecture can't force people to connect, it can only plan the crossing points, remove barriers, and make the meeting places useful and attractive.

Denise Scott Brown (1931–)

Of course you condition perception through a building but you must be careful not to overdo it, otherwise you asphyxiate the user. It is necessary to find the right balance between the control of the experience of space, and a freedom which allows things to happen.

Alvaro Siza (1933–)

I STARTED OUT TRYING TO
CREATE BUILDINGS THAT
WOULD SPARKLE LIKE ISOLATED
JEWELS; NOW I WANT THEM
TO CONNECT, TO FORM
A NEW KIND OF LANDSCAPE,
TO FLOW TOGETHER WITH
CONTEMPORARY CITIES AND THE
LIVES OF THEIR PEOPLES.

Zaha Hadid (1950–)

I always consider a building as part of the whole, a piece which creates **a collective performance,** *which is the city.*

Christian de Portzamparc (1944–)

ANY WORK OF ARCHITECTURE WHICH DOES NOT EXPRESS SERENITY IS A MISTAKE.

Luis Barragán (1902–88)

THE ARCHITECTURE WE REMEMBER IS THAT WHICH **NEVER CONSOLES OR COMFORTS US.**

Peter Eisenman (1932–)

In a strange way,
architecture is really
an unfinished thing,
because even though
the building is finished,
it takes on a new life.
It becomes part of
a new dynamic: how
people will occupy it,
use it, think about it.

Daniel Libeskind (1946–)

The greatest satisfaction, I think, is when a building opens and the public **possesses it** and you cut the umbilical cord and you see it taking on its own life. There's no greater satisfaction.

Moshe Safdie (1938–)

You have to
have endurance
in this profession.
You start a project
as a young
person and then
at the end you
are another
person. You are
ready to go
for your pension.

Santiago Calatrava (1951–)

What you newspaper and magazine writers, who work in rabbit time, don't understand is that **the practice of architecture has to be measured in elephant time.**

Eero Saarinen (1910–61)

I am an architect who builds, and therefore I am an optimist. Being an optimist is a prerequisite for anybody who wants to build, because **construction is a matter of optimism**; it's a matter of facing the future with confidence.

Cesar Pelli (1926–)

I am not optimistic or pessimistic. I feel that optimism and pessimism are very unbalanced. I am a very hard engineer. I am a mechanic. I am a sailor. I am an air pilot. I don't tell people I can get you across the ocean with my ship unless I know what I'm talking about.

Buckminster Fuller (1895–1983)

THE BUILDING ITSELF
STANDS ALONE, IN
COMPLETE SOLITUDE–
NO MORE POLEMICAL
STATEMENTS, NO
MORE TROUBLES.
IT HAS ACQUIRED ITS
DEFINITIVE CONDITION
AND WILL REMAIN
ALONE FOREVER,
MASTER OF ITSELF.

Rafael Moneo (1937–)

WHAT MOTIVATES
ME IS WORK ON
DISAPPEARANCE, ON
THE LIMITS BETWEEN
A PRESENCE AND
AN ABSENCE OF THE
ARCHITECTURE.

Dominique Perrault (1953–)

Architecture is a practice of amnesia. When projects are completed, the numerous ideas, thoughts, and research that supported their making are most often purged as the project is narrowed down to its essence—typically leaving behind only a set of final photographs and, maybe, a single sketch.

Jeanne Gang (1964–)

In reality some images or drawings have a greater impact than many buildings that are built.

Emilio Ambasz (1943–)

The building has not means
of locomotion, it cannot hide itself,
it cannot get away. There it is,
and there it will stay–**telling more
truths about him who made it,**
who thought it, than he in his
fatuity imagines; revealing his mind
and his heart exactly for what
they are worth, not a whit more,
not a whit less.

Louis Sullivan (1856–1924)

It is not right to take one building out of the whole work of a man because even the faults show the changes in his work. They show the humanity of the man that did it.

Enrico Peressutti (1908–76)

Architecture is a discipline that takes time and patience. If one spends enough years writing complex novels one might be able, someday, to construct a respectable haiku.

Thom Mayne (1944–)

I like ruins because
what remains is not
the total design,
but the clarity of thought,
the naked structure,
the spirit of the thing.

Tadao Ando (1941–)

MY WORK IS A
CONSTANT PROCESS
OF UNCOVERING.
DO NOT FORGET,
THERE IS NO NEW
HISTORY. THE
ARCHITECTS I AM
GOING BACK TO ARE
ALL STILL THERE.
THEY DO NOT MOVE.
I MOVE.

Peter Eisenman (1932–)

We don't have preconceived ideas; we work, we analyze, we read, we step into projects knowing that we're not the first ones there.

Elizabeth Diller (1954–)

The destiny of human beings, as I see it, is to experience the world they inhabit—the universe inhabited by the immense scope of the human mind—and to construct that experience, that reality, in works of uncompromised energy, **unrestrained by fear.**

Lebbeus Woods (1940–)

Now I know why acknowledgment pages can go on for so long. Although my name is on the cover, this book is scarcely the work of one. First and foremost, I must thank my editor, Sara Bader: this would be nowhere near the elegant volume you hold if not for her experience, dedication, and insight. I would also like to thank Princeton Architectural Press for taking a chance on an unknown quantity. And to Paul Wagner and Jan Haux who designed *The Architect Says*. Their thoughtful and creative treatment of the text has truly made the book a visual feast. To my colleagues at NBBJ, who are an amazing group of professionals, from whom I have learned so much. And finally, always, for Ed and Jacob.

Think well to the end, consider the end first.

Leonardo da Vinci (1452–1519)